A long time ago
many animals and plants
were very different
from those we see today.

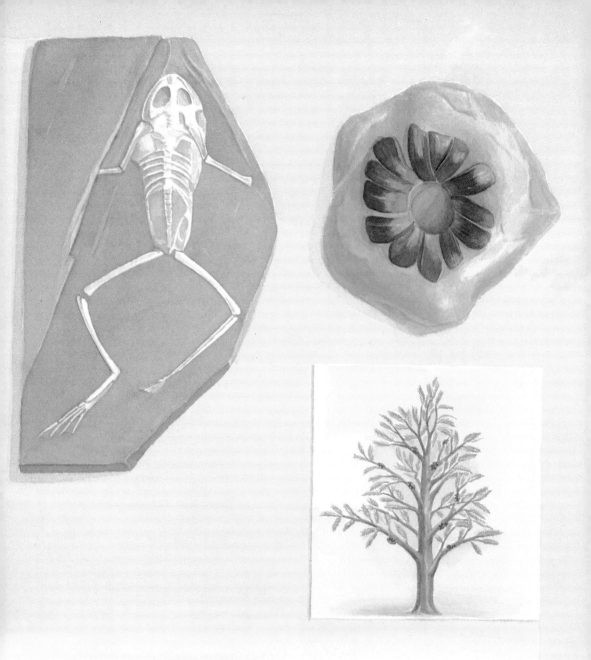

In very old rocks
there are fossils
of plants and animals
that lived long ago.

Do you think these 'sea-lilies' are flowers?

No, they are animals
that lived in the sea.
They caught tiny creatures
with their waving arms.

Some little creatures are found in amber.

Amber was once gum
oozing from pine trees.
The creatures were trapped in it!

Mammoths are now extinct but
we know what they looked like.

Long ago, some fell into deep holes.
They were frozen.

Fossil plants and animals
can show us that a land was once
hotter than it is today.

These African animals used to live
in Britain.

In the Ice Age, parts of Europe
were much colder than they are now.
Mammoths lived there with other creatures
that live in the Arctic today.

We can find out which trees grew
a long time ago.

Long after the trees have died
tree pollen can be found in wet ground
like the dark peat in the picture.
Sometimes we find trees, too.
This birch tree was cut down with a flint tool.

Hazel

Pine

Oak

   If we look at the pollen
through a microscope
we can see different pollen grains.
We can tell what kind of tree
the pollen came from.
So we know what trees grew
a long time ago.

There were no trees in the Ice Age.
When the ice melted
birch and pine were the first trees to grow.

The weather became warmer
so more kinds of trees could grow.
The first farmers in Northern Europe
found trees like the ones
we can see today.

Archaeologists can find out what crops
the farmers used to grow.
When the farmers made pots
seeds often stuck in the clay.

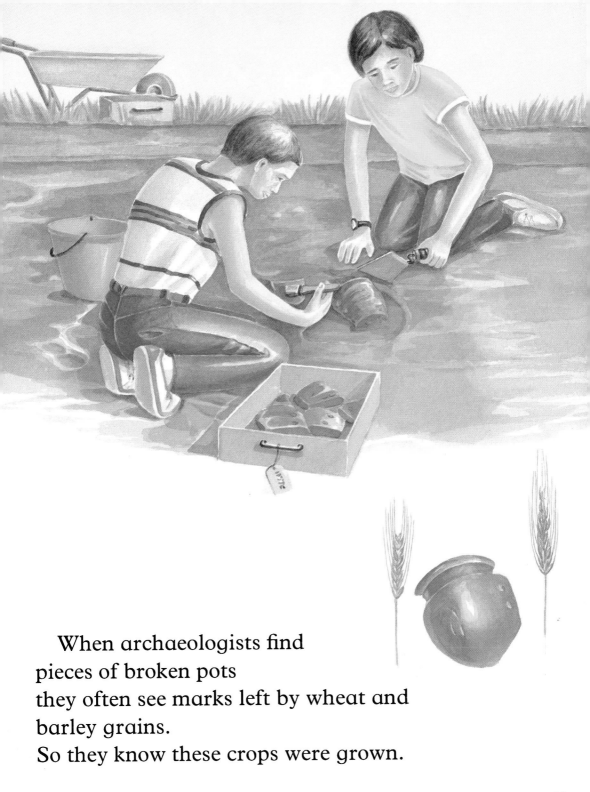

When archaeologists find
pieces of broken pots
they often see marks left by wheat and
barley grains.
So they know these crops were grown.

Archaeologists also look for
the bones of animals
that were eaten long ago.

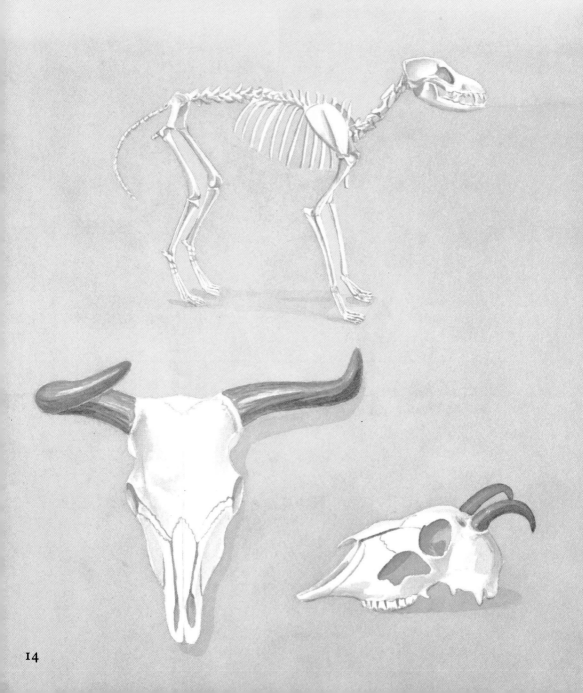

They have found out
what animals were kept on farms long ago.
Farmers kept sheep, goats, pigs and cows.
Dogs helped to herd them.

Do you think this is a fossil
of a calf's head?

No, it is a natural stone,
but it is very lifelike!